Bicycles

Written by Sandra Iversen

People have been riding bicycles
for a very long time.
Bicycles have always had wheels.
They have always had pedals.
They have always had handlebars.
They have always had a seat,
that some people call a saddle.
But bicycles have not always had brakes
and gears.

handlebars

wheel

seat

pedal

brakes

gears

3

Old-Fashioned Bicycles

Old-fashioned bicycles were very simple.
They did not have brakes and gears.
Some had one big wheel
and one little wheel.
People call these bicycles, penny-farthings.

Some old-fashioned cycles
had three wheels.
People call these, tricycles.
Some old-fashioned tricycles
were as big as bicycles with two wheels.

Some old-fashioned cycles
had one wheel.
People call these, unicycles.

You can still see people
riding penny-farthings and unicycles, today.

penny-farthing

Bicycles for Work

Some people use bicycles
to help them with their work.
They use bicycles to carry things.
They fix a basket or a tray
onto the bicycle.
Some of these cycles have two wheels.
Some of them have three wheels.
Some people put seats on the back.
They carry people around in the seats.

basket

tray

7

Bicycles for Fun

Some people use bicycles for fun.
These bicycles have gears and brakes.
Some of these bicycles are little
so people are able to do tricks on them.
They go up and down ramps.
They jump in the air.
Sometimes, they take a tumble.

Some people have fun
racing down the street.
Some people have fun
riding in the water.

Some riders fly high in the air.

Some riders take a tumble.

9

Bicycles for Speed and Fitness

Some people have bicycles
that are made for racing.
These bicycles are able to go very fast
when people pedal fast.
Some people race these bicycles
on the road.
Some people race on a track.

Some people pedal fast and go nowhere.
They are riding stationary bicycles.
They are going nowhere,
but they are getting fit.

People get fit no matter what kind of bicycle they are riding.

Index